The Maya

by Robert Nicholson

Editorial consultant: Tim Laughton,
Department of Art History, University of Essex

TWO-CAN

First published in Great Britain in 1993 by
Two-Can Publishing Ltd
346 Old Street
London EC1V 9NQ
in association with
Scholastic Publications Ltd

Printed and bound in Hong Kong

2 4 6 8 10 9 7 5 3 1

A catalogue record for this book is available from
the British Library

PBK ISBN: 1-85434-213-4
HBK ISBN:1-85434-212-6

Photographic credits
Ancient Art and Architecture Collection: p12, p30 (right);
E.T. Archive: p14; Eye Ubiquitous: p23 (right);
Werner Forman: p7 (right), p10, p13, p15, p16, p21;
Tony Morrison: p5, p30 (left)

Illustration credits
Mei-Yim Low: pp4-24 Maxine Hamil: cover, pp25-29

Contents

All words marked in **bold** are explained in
the glossary.

Chichen Itza
•

• Uxmal

Gulf of Mexico

YUCATAN

• Palenque

• Tikal

Bonampak •

GUATEMALA

• Quiriga

• Copan

Pacific Ocean

▼ The ruins of the classic Maya city of Palenque still lie amongst the tree-covered hills of southern Mexico.

The Maya World

The Maya have lived in Central America for thousands of years, mainly in the areas we now call Guatemala and Mexico. Between 200 and 900AD, when their **civilization** was at its peak, they built magnificent cities and temples. They became expert in mathematics, science and **astronomy**. They also made books and were the only Central American people at the time to do so.

Around 1000AD, the Maya way of life changed and people left most of the great cities, returning to villages deep in the jungle. When explorers arrived from Europe in the sixteenth century, they found only the remains of a civilization which had clearly once been great. The decline of the Maya cities is a mystery and no one knows for sure what happened. Eventually most were abandoned and their ruins remained hidden in the jungle for hundreds of years.

Today, descendants of the ancient Maya still live in Yucatan and Guatemala.

Forest and Scrubland

The lands where the Maya lived were covered with forest, bushes and grass. In the south lay high mountains and thick tropical rainforests. In the north, on the Yucatan Peninsula, bush and scrub grew thickly. The weather was usually warm and in the rainforest it was very hot and humid.

There was plenty of rain so the ground was fertile and crops grew easily. Farming in the forest was simple and most Maya people were farmers. They only needed to work on their land for about 50 days of each year. For the rest of the time they were free to help their relatives and neighbours and to serve their rulers. Men worked together in teams to build the huge temples and palaces of the cities and look after the roads which linked them.

▼ Maya farmers cut down and burnt the trees and bushes to make clearings in the forest. Here they prepared fields, planted crops and built cities and villages. This kind of farming is called **slash and burn** and is still used today.

Hunting

Yucatan was known as 'the land of turkey and deer' and the Maya were keen hunters. They found many kinds of animals on the peninsula to hunt and eat, including deer, turkeys, pigs and large rodents called agoutis.

They used traps and snares to catch small animals and blowguns to shoot birds. Bigger animals were killed with clubs or bows and arrows and hunters had packs of dogs to help them. The Maya also fished, using nets or hooks and lines to catch fish in the rivers and sea.

▲ The Maya did not have any metal tools. They made elaborate flint tools like this one for decoration at their ceremonies. For clearing the forest they had simple stone cutting tools.

Farms and Farmers

Maya farmers had their own plots of land and gardens next to their houses. Each village also had a plot of communal land which everyone would help to look after.

In swampy areas farmers drained the swamps, enclosed them with earth banks to keep the water out and planted crops there. Then they built **irrigation** canals which brought water from the swamps to the crops growing in the fields.

The Maya made use of several kinds of trees. Cocoa beans came from cacao trees. They were considered valuable and were sometimes used as money. People chewed the leaves of sapodilla trees and copal trees gave a resin used in religious ceremonies.

▲ Can you recognize any of the crops from the picture opposite growing in this village plot? The farmers in the distance are tending the maize, while women pick the other vegetables and fruit.

The Farming Year

Farmers cut down and burnt trees and bushes during the dry season, from August until about October. They also burnt any trees that were too large to cut down. The ashes left behind were good for the soil, although it gradually became less fertile after it had been used for a few years.

They planted crops in May, as the rainy season was starting. Then the only real jobs were weeding and preparing next year's plot. Crops were harvested in November.

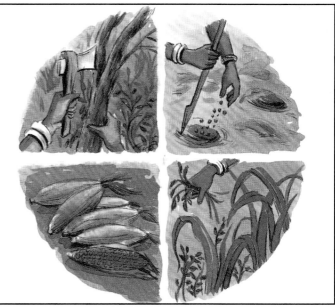

Corn or maize was the most important crop for the Maya. It grew easily and in large quantities. Farmers also grew other crops such as beans, **squash**, sweet potatoes and cotton, as well as fruits such as papaya. However, if a corn crop failed it could cause a famine in the area, since corn was the main ingredient of most Maya meals.

water-melon

papaya

corn or maize

beans

avocado

chillies

Nobles, Freemen and Slaves

There were many Maya cities, each one ruled by its own chief or leader called the **halach uinic**. He had complete control over the people of his city and all the surrounding villages. When he died, his power passed to his eldest son.

Although the cities traded with one another, they also spent a lot of time at war. When they were not fighting, rulers tried to show that they were more important than their neighbours by building bigger temples and palaces.

Maya farmers were **freemen**. They lived in villages outside the cities and worked in teams with their family and friends to farm the land. There were no horses or cattle to carry loads so noble families had slaves to do the heavy work. These slaves were often enemies who had been captured in war, or criminals being punished.

▼ Halach uinics were **absolute rulers**. They had total power but were advised by a **council of state** made up of local nobles or lords.

▲ **Batabs** helped the halach uinic to rule. They collected taxes and acted as judges in local disputes and leaders in times of war.

Houses had no doors and a simple screen or blanket hung over the entrance.

The house was divided into two sections. The front half was for cooking and eating. The back half was for sleeping.

People slept on raised racks made from wood and woven bark.

The hearth and fire for cooking were in the middle of the front room. The smoke went straight up through the roof.

A Maya House

Most Maya lived in tiny, simple houses. These were made from whatever materials people could find easily, usually rough stone, wood or woven twigs. Roofs were thatched with palm leaves or grass and were usually pitched high so that rain water would drain off easily. People also built houses on small mounds so that they were protected from flood waters.

Often several houses were arranged around a small square. They probably belonged to members of the same family.

When someone died, their body was placed under the floor of their house. It was covered with red powder, wrapped in a layer of matting and then buried with jewellery and food.

The Maya kept a number of animals, including dogs. Some were bred for hunting and others just for eating, such as a special hairless dog which could be cooked without skinning, like a pig.

Cities and Temples

The Maya built splendid cities with huge pyramids, temples and palaces. Roads ran from one city to another and were used for big processions during important ceremonies. The temples were either covered with white **stucco** and polished so that they shone in the sun, or painted bright red or blue. They had raised tops to make them as tall as possible and were up to 70m (over 200ft) high. Sometimes a new temple was built around an old one, making an extra layer. Nobles and priests were the only Maya who actually lived in the cities. They spent much of their time in the small, dark rooms of the palaces.

▼ Priests carried out ceremonies in the temples. This priest is sacrificing an enemy captured in war.

▲ The Maya's favourite game was called **pok-a-tok**. It was played in the cities in long, thin courts surrounded by stepped stone walls where large crowds could sit and watch. These spectators placed bets and often lost all their clothes and jewellery to the winning team.

Pyramids and temples were arranged around plazas which were filled with large, upright stones called **stelae**. These were covered with the dates of important events and ceremonies and were rather like calendars or local notice boards.

▲ Pok-a-tok players wore heavy padding so that they would not be injured when they hit the ball. Their protection included a belt which was probably made from wood or leather.

Pok-A-Tok

Pok-a-tok games were often played as an important part of religious ceremonies, when some players were sacrificed to the gods. The players tried to hit a large, solid and very bouncy rubber ball through a stone ring. They were only allowed to use their elbows, forearms, hips or knees. The ring was mounted on one wall of the court, up to 10m (over 30ft) high, so it was very difficult to score. Some courts also had sloped playing surfaces. There was a complex scoring system and rules which historians still do not fully understand.

Religion and the Maya Gods

▼ People offered gifts to their gods by throwing precious objects into wells called **cenote**.

Religion played a major part in Maya life. People prayed every day to ask for success in whatever they might be doing and worshipped over 150 different gods. There was one for each important aspect of daily life. One of the chief gods was called Itzamna, which means 'Lizard House'. The Maya believed that he had invented writing, which they considered to be very important. There was another god for fishermen and even one for tattooing. People made many sacrifices to please their gods. These included slaves and enemies they had captured in war.

▲ The priests burned incense in special clay bowls to perfume the air during religious ceremonies. The incense was often made from copal resin or sometimes even from rubber.

Music and Dancing

The Maya loved dancing and making music . They had over 5,000 dances. These were part of huge religious ceremonies, which many people joined in. Their names (like 'The Monkey' and 'The Centipede') usually came from the animals that represented the gods. Musicians played wooden flutes, trumpets made from wood, clay or sea shells, and drums made from turtle shells.

Priests

There were a great many Maya priests. The high priests or **ah kin** were the most important. Some sat on the councils of state and advised on their important decisions. Others tried to predict or 'divine' the future. When a priest made a sacrifice, he was helped by another official called a nacom. People asked priests to help with the smallest problem. They had special jobs like conducting ceremonies or telling farmers when to plant their crops.

Writing

The Maya developed their own system of writing. No other ancient Central American people had a system that could be used to form full sentences and write stories. Maya words were not written with letters but with a complex system of pictures called **hieroglyphs**, each with its own meaning. Some represented whole words and a sentence or a story could be made by drawing several pictures together. The Maya covered their cities and buildings with hieroglyphs, which were carved into the stone. Most Maya could read some of the hieroglyphs, although priests and nobles were probably the only people who knew them all.

▶ This stone carving shows a Maya noblewoman writing.

Hieroglyphs

Here are some Maya words written as hieroglyphs:

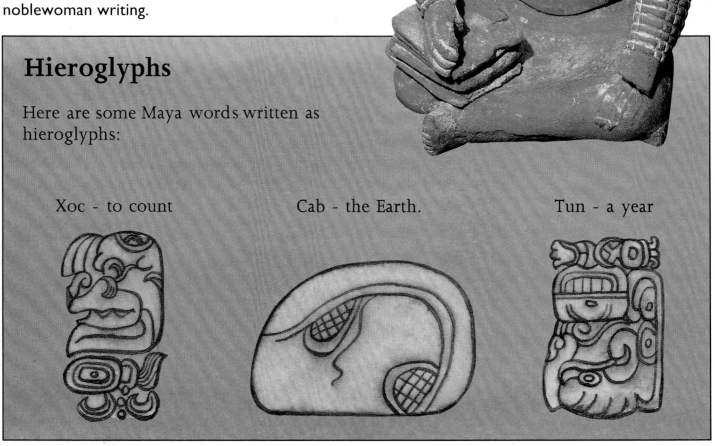

Xoc - to count   Cab - the Earth.   Tun - a year

16

The Maya also wrote in books made from the soft inner bark of a type of fig-tree. Each book was written on one long strip of bark which was folded over and over to form pages. The pens were quills made from turkey feathers. Only four Maya books have survived. The rest have been lost or were destroyed. When the first European explorers arrived in Central America in the sixteenth century, Christian missionaries came with them. They wanted to change the religion of the Maya people and thought that they could do so by burning Maya books.

▼ Stelae were covered with hieroglyphs which recorded important dates for local people. They often covered the life of one ruler and recorded the events of his reign. A new stela would sometimes be carved and put up to celebrate the end of a 20-year period.

▲ Hieroglyphs in a Maya book or codex were painted in black and red. Sometimes the background was brightly coloured.

Counting and Calendars

To write their numbers, the Maya used a system of dots, lines and shell pictures. They had zero, which was unusual in number systems at the time and made mathematics much easier. They counted using various combinations of the three signs. By writing a sign in a different position they gave it a different value. This is like our counting system, where 1 means one unit and 10 means one ten and no units, for example.

The Maya also used their skill in numbers and mathematics to work out calendars. They calculated how long it took the Earth to go around the Sun and the Moon to go around the Earth. They knew exactly how long a year was and their calculations were almost as precise as those produced by today's scientists and computers.

▲ Priests and nobles used their knowledge of calendars and astronomy for many of the rituals which were important in Maya life.

Number Signs

The Maya used only three signs to count:

0   1   5

All other numbers were made up using these signs:

4   7   10   19

Just as we move our signs across one column for numbers over nine...

1 0

(1 x 10) (0 x 1)

... the Maya moved their signs up one line for numbers over 19. So 20 was written:

•   (1 x 20)

(0 x 1)

When they reached 399

(19 x 20)

(19 x 1)

the signs moved up another line: •

(1 x 400)

(0 x 20)

(0 x 1)

Can you write your age and the number of people in your family using the Maya system? Try the number of pupils in your school, too.

Calendars

The Maya could work out when the weather would be best for planting or harvesting crops. They knew when eclipses of the Sun and Moon were going to happen and even worked out how long the planet Venus took to go around the Sun.

They had several ways of counting the days and years. One was a ritual calendar called the **tzolkin**. The days were given one of 20 names and a number from one to 13. It took 260 days (20x13) for the first day to come round again. Another was the **haab** year. There were 20 days in a month, which was called a uinal. Eighteen uinals made a year or a tun. This added up to 360 days. The Maya then added five more days to make 365, as we have today. The extra days were believed to be unlucky.

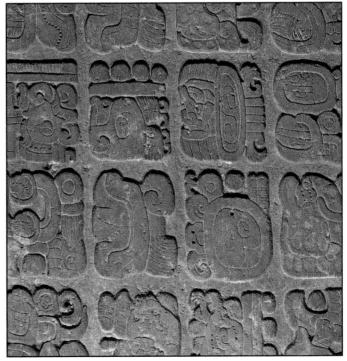

▲ Calendar stones were carved with a series of hieroglyphs which recorded important dates.

19

Families and Children

The members of a Maya family usually lived together in the same village. Boys helped their fathers in the fields and learnt all about farming. From the age of four or five, they did not live at home but stayed in communal houses with others of the same age. Girls stayed with their mothers, learning how to cook and look after the house and family. They were taught to spin, weave and make clothes.

The Maya had four names each: a private name, given by their parents, a public nickname to be used by everyone and names from both their father's and their mother's families to make sure that when two people married, they were not related.

▼ Women worked at home, spinning and weaving cotton and coarser agave fibre, making pottery and growing and preparing food.

Mayan Craft

Jade was the most valuable material that the Maya knew. They used the hard, green stone to carve beautiful masks, jewellery and statues. They also carved statues from other kinds of stone and modelled terracotta figures.

▶ Women used weaving looms with one end fixed and the other held in position by a belt worn around their hips.

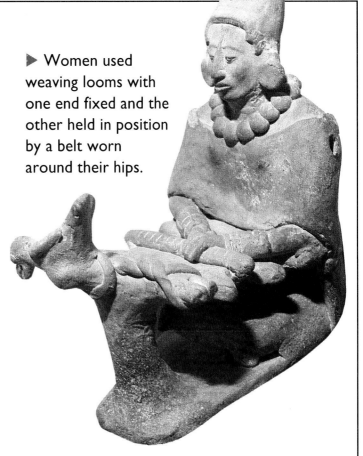

◀ Maya women and girls were expert potters and made many household items such as cooking pots and plates. They used coiled clay, smoothed with a special tool and decorated with brightly painted human shapes, animals and hieroglyphs. The most popular colours were orange, black, red and grey.

When boys were about 14, their parents set about choosing a bride for them. They took great care to make sure that the couple were not closely related and were helped by professional matchmakers called **at atanzahob**. Once the bride had been chosen, which could take a year or more, the marriage took place. Girls were usually 14 or 15 and boys slightly older.

A wedding ceremony lasted several days. There were important prayers and rituals to make sure that the gods would bless the marriage. The bride's and groom's horoscopes were checked by a priest to make sure that they were suited. Usually the husband's family gave the bride's family a present of new clothes. Once married, a man often built a new house near to his wife's family house and worked for his father-in-law for a few years. Only then was he allowed to move away and build a larger house for his own family.

Clothes and Beauty

The Maya were much shorter than most people today. Men were usually about 1.5m (under 5ft) tall and women slightly shorter. They were stocky and strong.

Their clothes were very simple – the weather was mostly warm so they did not need much protection from the cold. Men wore a loincloth, a band of material that was wound around the waist and between the legs. Women wore a **huipil**, a smock-like dress made from one length of cloth with short sleeves and a hole cut for the head. Most Maya wore leather sandals or moccasins. Some may have dipped their feet into latex to make simple rubber shoes. If the weather did get cold, men and women both wore a kind of cloak called a manta. This could also be used as a blanket at night and even hung in the entrance of a house as a makeshift door.

Fashion

It was fashionable for Maya people to have elongated and flattened heads and to be cross-eyed. To change the shape of their heads while their skulls were still very soft, babies had wooden frames strapped to them. To make a child cross-eyed, a bead was tied so that it dangled just in front of the eyes.

▼ Large noses were a sign of nobility. Nobles often wore these strangely shaped clay covers on their noses to show how important they were. Some nobles also wore nose studs with jewels in them. Men wore

their hair pulled back and burnt a bare spot in the back of their heads. People sometimes filed down their front teeth into points and filled the gaps with pieces of jade.

▲ Even those Maya who wore very simple clothes decorated themselves with jewellery such as necklaces, earrings and wristlets.

Tattooing was very popular — men often had tattoos all over their faces. Men and women painted their faces and bodies. For unmarried men the colour was black; for unmarried women, red; priests used blue, warriors red and black and slaves black with white stripes.

Food

Corn was the Maya's main food and was part of almost every meal. In the morning people often ate **saka'**, a kind of porridge made of corn with chilli peppers. When they were working in the fields they would take **tamales** with them. These were corn dough dumplings with meat or vegetables inside, wrapped in leaves from the corn plant. The big meal came in the early evening. Usually it included **tortillas**, with a spicy meat or bean stew, squash and sweet potatoes. The Maya kept stingless bees to make honey for sweetening food and drinks. They mixed it with bark to make balche, a powerful alcoholic drink used in religious ceremonies.

▲ Tortillas were made from ground corn mixed with water and cooked on clay platters.

Spicy Bean Stew

Ingredients

I tin of kidney beans ● 4 cloves of garlic, crushed ● 2 bay leaves ● I tablespoon cooking oil ● I onion, chopped finely ¹/₂ teaspoon chilli powder ● I tablespoon tomato puree

● Drain the beans and simmer them in 500ml fresh water with half the garlic and half the oil until they are soft (about 15 minutes).
● Strain the beans and keep the water.
● Gently fry the onion in the remaining oil until it is soft, then add the rest of the garlic, chilli powder, bay leaves and tomato puree and cook for a few more minutes, stirring well.
● Add the beans and 250ml of the water and cook gently in the frying pan for about 15 minutes, then season.

Make sure you ask an adult to help you with the chopping and cooking.

The Hero Twins' Revenge

Like many people over the centuries, the Maya told special stories to help explain things they did not fully understand about the world around them. This tale tells us how the rabbit and the deer came to have such short tails.

Long ago, in the high mountains of the southern Maya lands, there lived four brothers. They belonged to a noble family and were grandsons of the gods. Hunahpu and Xbalanque, the youngest, were brave warriors and became known as the Hero Twins. Their elder brothers were corn farmers who looked after the family's land. They were very jealous of the twins and played tricks on them, but this made Hunahpu and Xbalanque angry and one day they decided to teach the older boys a lesson. In a flash, they had turned them into monkeys, scampering about among the trees. Of course they could no longer work on the land and grow the family's food, so although farming was not their favourite job, the Hero Twins agreed to help out.

One morning, when the weather was just right, they decided that the time had come to start work. Next year's corn crop needed planting, but first they had to clear a patch

of land in the forest and prepare the field.
So they swung their axe, pick and
blowguns onto their shoulders and set out.
As they went, they called back to their
grandmother, who stood in the doorway
waving them off.

"We'll have our lunch in the fields today.
Would you bring it for us, Grandmother?"

"Of course. I'll be there at midday – look
out for me!" she replied, waving them off.

Soon Hunahpu and Xbalanque arrived at
the spot they wanted to clear for planting.
They drove their pick into the ground and
their axe into the trunk of the nearest tree.
As soon as they let go of them, the tools
began working on their own, as if by magic,
chopping down scrub, felling trees and
digging up the earth. The brothers were

delighted. Now they could spend the morning shooting their blowguns and enjoying themselves! But first they said to a turtledove sitting in a nearby tree, "If you see our grandmother coming with our lunch, start singing as loud as you can. We don't want her to catch us enjoying ourselves while our tools do all the work!"

At the stroke of midday, the dove began to sing. Hunahpu and Xbalanque quickly grabbed handfuls of earth, rubbing it onto their faces and arms. Then they took hold

of their pick and axe and pretended to be tired from a hard morning's work.

"You poor boys, you look quite worn out!" said their grandmother, handing them an enormous basket of maize dumplings and tortillas. They gobbled up the meal greedily and said that they would soon be home as they were too tired to do much more work. When they left the field, it was completely cleared and all ready for planting.

The following day, they returned to the field with seeds and dibble sticks. They were

amazed to see that during the night, the field had become overgrown with thick, jungly plants. It looked just as it had when they arrived there the previous day.

"Who has been playing tricks on us?" asked Hunahpu angrily.

"Whoever it was, they must have been busy all night spoiling what we did yesterday," replied Xbalanque.

They put their tools straight back to work and by the end of the day, as if by magic, the field was ready for planting again.

"We can't have anyone making fools of us like that again," the twins agreed as they walked home. "We must return to the field tonight to find out who was the culprit. We'll give them quite a surprise."

They waited until darkness fell, then crept back and hid behind some scrubby bushes at the side of the field. Just after midnight, they heard the sound of footsteps approaching. They strained their ears and peered through the bushes to see who it was.

Strange voices seemed to be murmuring in the darkness, "Rise up trees! Rise up vines!" As the sounds grew louder, the twins saw a

huge army of animals marching towards them across the cleared field. And as they went, they were ordering plants to grow up in the field yet again. There were all kinds of forest animals and each was speaking its own language. But as grandsons of the gods, Hunahpu and Xbalanque had special powers and could understand every word the animals were saying. They were determined to catch these mischievous creatures. Reaching out from behind the bushes, they tried to grab each one as it passed. But the first to go by, the jaguar and the puma, were much too fast and bounded off into the undergrowth.

Next came the rabbit and the deer. The brothers snatched at them and just managed to catch their long, flowing tails.

"Got you!" they cried. "We'll teach you to spoil our land." But to their surprise, both tails came off in their hands as the frightened creatures sprang away.

The animals never returned to the field and the Hero Twins were finally able to plant their corn. But to this day, deer and rabbits always have short, stumpy little tails.

How We Know

Ancient Maya cities and villages were covered by the jungle for hundreds of years. Have you ever wondered how we can find out about the people who lived there so long ago?

Evidence from around us

There are still two million Maya living in Central America. Slash and burn is still the most widely used method of farming. Some priests still use the ancient calendar systems.

▲ Maya people in Central America today still live in traditional houses. These are very similar to their ancestors' homes.

Evidence from the ground

After the Maya civilization declined at the end of the Classic period, the rainforest grew over many cities and buildings. But archaeologists are now discovering more and more that can tell us about the Maya. Recent discoveries have helped people to decipher and understand more of the hieroglyphs. Jewels and riches are still being found in tombs and many have recently been dredged up from cenotes.

▲ Tikal is one of the largest Maya sites. It has the remains of several temples and stelae are still standing in this city plaza.

In 1839, two explorers – an American called John Stephens and an Englishman named Frederick Catherwood – found the hidden city of Copan, which has since told us much about the Maya.

Evidence from books

In 1562 Bishop Landa, a Spanish priest, burnt many of the Maya books. He said that they contained 'nothing but superstition and lies of the devil'. Many more books have been lost or have rotted away in the humid atmosphere of the forest. Only four survive today. This has left us with few written records of the ancient Maya way of life and made it more difficult to decipher the hieroglyphs. Maya Indians do not use the same system of writing today.

The decline of the Maya cities is still a mystery. Some historians believe that farmers found it difficult to grow enough food as the number of people grew. This may have led to more wars between the cities as they fought over land.

Glossary

absolute ruler
Person who can rule without having to consult others.

ah kin
High priest.

astronomy
Study of the planets, the stars and their movements.

at atanzahob
Matchmaker whose job was arranging marriages.

batab
Local lord who collected taxes for the ruler, and sat on the council of state.

cenote
Well formed naturally in limestone rock.

civilization
Organized society with its own culture, government and laws.

council of state
Group of the most important nobles and batabs who helped the halach uinic rule.

freemen
Men who were not nobles, priests or slaves but who owned land.

haab
Maya year of 18 months, each 20 days long.

halach uinic
Maya ruler or chief.

hieroglyph
Picture symbol used instead of a letter or word in writing.

huipil
Short-sleeved dress, like a smock, worn by women.

irrigation
Method of supplying water to crops using man-made canals and ditches.

pok-a-tok
Maya ball game played with hips, knees and elbows.

saka'
Kind of porridge made from corn and chilli peppers.

slash and burn
Method of farming, usually in tropical rainforests, where a plot is cleared and burnt before crops are planted.

squash
Family of vegetables that includes marrows.

stela
Large upright stone carved with hieroglyphs.

stucco
Fine, shiny plaster made from ground limestone.

tamale
Corn dough dumpling with meat or vegetables.

tortilla (Spanish word - the Maya word is unknown)
A flat corn pancake.

tzolkin
Calendar of 13 months, each twenty days long.

Index